FORWARD SKILLS

GARETH EDWARDS
WITH IAN ROBERTSON

STANLEY PAUL
London Melbourne Sydney Auckland Johannesburg

ACKNOWLEDGMENTS

I should like to thank Ian Robertson once again for all his help in the preparation of this book, all the Pontypool players who kindly agreed to demonstrate their particular skills, especially Bobby Windsor, Terry Cobner and Jeff Squire, and also Allan Martin who travelled from Aberavan to demonstrate line-out techniques. I would also like to thank Colin Elsey of Colorsport for taking such excellent photos during the special sessions at Pontypool and also for providing all the outstanding action pictures from international matches which have been used in this book.

Stanley Paul & Co. Ltd

An imprint of the Hutchinson Publishing Group

3 Fitzroy Square, London W1P 6JD

Hutchinson Group (Australia) Pty Ltd
30–32 Cremorne Street, Richmond South, Victoria 3121
PO Box 151, Broadway, New South Wales 2007

Hutchinson (NZ) Ltd
32–34 View Road, PO Box 40–086, Glenfield, Auckland 10

Hutchinson Group (SA) (Pty) Ltd
PO Box 337, Bergvlei 2012, South Africa

First published 1980

© Gareth Edwards 1980

Set in Monophoto Univers Light by
Willmer Brothers Ltd, Birkenhead, Merseyside

Printed in Great Britain by The Anchor Press Ltd,
Tiptree, Essex

ISBN 0 09 142610 3 cased
     0 09 142611 1 paper

CONTENTS

Introduction 5

1 The set-scrum 7
  Hooker 7
  Front row 10
  Locks 10
  Back row 13
  Channel one possession 14
  Channel two possession 16
  Opposition put-in 17
  Back-row moves 18

2 The ruck and maul 25
  The ruck 26
  The maul 30
  Rolling maul 36
  Falling on the ball 38

3 The line-out 41
  The throw-in 42
  Jumping techniques 44
  Two-handed catch 46
  Palming 50
  Two-handed catch at the front 51
  Short throw to the front 52
  The peel 54
  Two-man line-out 58
  Throw over the top 60

INTRODUCTION

In 1979, I wrote my first coaching book called *Rugby Skills*, which dealt with all the basic individual skills that I felt every young player should know about. I put in to that book all the experience and knowledge I had gained during twelve years of international rugby with Wales and the British Lions. I thought that book was essential reading for every player whether he was a back or a forward, because during the course of a game any one of the thirty players might be called on to catch a high kick, give a scoring pass, put in a crucial relieving kick to touch or pull off a match-saving tackle. I stressed in the introduction to *Rugby Skills* that a practical knowledge of the game's fundamental skills was of paramount importance if full enjoyment and satisfaction were to be derived from rugby.

In preparing this second book, which I believe to be a natural companion volume, I have written a book that will be of much greater, but not I hope exclusive, interest to the forwards. In the same way the first volume dealt with all the game's individual skills and was perhaps of greater relevance to the backs, I trust this volume will restore the balance by explaining all the basic skills which every forward should understand and try to master.

Backs should be just as interested in the chapter on rucking and mauling as they may often set up, or be involved in, a ruck or maul. The chapters on the scrum and the line-out are exclusively for budding young forwards.

I have been very fortunate to have played scrum-half behind the best set of forwards in the last twenty years – the 1974 British Lions pack. I write briefly about what made them the best pack in the world. I played behind great Welsh packs, especially in 1977 and 1978, and I write about their particular skills and the attacking opportunities they gave me and the very talented back division Wales had at that time.

Gareth Edwards about to pass after Wales have won good set-scrum possession against England in 1974

In this book I have tried to describe the vital ingredients which go to make up a great pack. To demonstrate the highly specialized techniques which each one of the eight forwards must try to learn I am delighted that I have had the assistance of some of my great friends from Welsh and Lions teams of recent years.

No one knows more about front-row play than Bobby Windsor. Bobby demonstrates all the hooker's basic skills and describes the role of the props in the set-scrum. Allan Martin has proved himself one of the top line-out exponents in modern rugby and he illustrates the various techniques every jumper should know about. And very few players in my time are better qualified to discuss rucking and mauling than Terry Cobner and Jeff Squire. With these four outstanding British Lions forwards, I examine the role of every forward in the set-scrum, in the loose and at the line-out.

I played behind one or two pretty moderate packs in my career as well and I also learned plenty from them! From that experience of playing behind beaten forwards, I try to point out the best methods to compete at the line-out if the opposition enjoy the luxury of two or even three taller jumpers. I mention what to do if the other side are heavier and stronger in the set-scrums; and in these special circumstances, how best your side can protect the ball in the loose.

I hope there is plenty for every forward to learn all he needs to know about the basic individual and collective, techniques of forward play.

Rugby is the greatest team game of all. It is crucial that all eight forwards understand exactly what they should each be doing in every situation, whether it is set piece or in the loose. They must all work together in complete harmony and it really is true to say that each pack is only as strong as its weakest link. The more practice a pack has together, the better it will become. To become as good as Bobby Windsor, Allan Martin, Terry Cobner or Jeff Squire is the end product of years of practice, hard graft and dedication. The good things of life don't come easily, but they are well worth working for. I hope this book with all its illustrations helps you on the road to success and also helps you to get the maximum fun and satisfaction from rugby.

1 THE SET-SCRUM

I have always placed tremendous emphasis on the importance of the set-scrum. No matter how talented a back division may be, there is very little they can achieve against a good side if their pack is being destroyed in the scrums. I've been very fortunate that throughout my career I played behind many outstanding packs. At club level Cardiff have produced good packs in the last ten years and Wales, with the possible exception of 1974 and 1975, have been as good at scrummaging as any country in the world. But to me three packs have stood out head and shoulders above the rest. The best club pack in the last few years – and with five British Lions in it that is no wonder – has been Pontypool. I'm delighted that some of their great players have agreed to demonstrate the basic skills in this book.

Secondly, the Welsh forwards from 1976 until 1978, when I retired, were so outstanding they presented me with three marvellous years of winning international rugby on which to end my career. But, without doubt, the best pack I have ever played behind or seen anywhere in the world was the 1974 British Lions Test pack. It had absolutely everything: two really strong, aggressive and brilliant scrummaging props in Ian McLauchlan and Fran Cotton, who could also ruck and maul and support at the line-out with the best of them; then there was Bobby Windsor, a great hooker and scrummager, and a tearaway in the loose. We had a perfect combination at lock in Willie John McBride and Gordon Brown; they were both completely dedicated scrummagers, incredible grafters in the loose, and tremendous at the line-out. If they didn't win the ball, then neither did the opposition. And what a back row. All three

The formidable and famous Pontypool, Wales and British Lions front row of Graham Price, Bobby Windsor and Charlie Faulkner

worked hard in the set-scrum. Mervyn Davies and Roger Uttley also contributed superb line-out ball and capitalized on the loose ball set up by Fergus Slattery, who was probably the fastest flanker of all time. I've never seen a better pack of forwards.

Those '74 Lions have set an incredibly high standard by which to judge all other packs and behind them I enjoyed many of the happiest and best moments of my rugby life. Their skills and techniques were as near to perfection as any side is ever likely to come. And with them it all started at the set-scrum. Just what those scrummaging techniques are we can examine now with the help of the Pontypool pack.

HOOKER

The hooker is the most important player in the team at a set-scrum on your own put-in, but the other seven forwards and the scrum-half all have crucial roles to play if you are to win good possession. The forwards must make sure the hooker is comfortable and not subjected to great pressure from the opposition so that he has a clear view of the ball coming into the tunnel and can give 100 per cent of his concentration to securing a quick, clean strike.

As a scrum-half, I must find out at what speed the hooker likes the ball to be fed into the scrum and how he likes to strike for the ball and I must make certain I do my best to comply with his wishes at every scrum. The timing between the scrum-half and hooker is vital; it is of paramount importance during a match for the scrum-half to make sure first of all that the scrum is steady and the hooker comfortable, and then to put the ball in at the same speed and in the same way at every scrum. The scrum-half must be consistent in his delivery.

At the end of a training session it is well worthwhile spending five minutes with the hooker practising the feed.

In this sequence, Bobby Windsor adopts his scrummaging position against a goal-post (1/1). His weight is almost all on his left leg with his right foot slightly further forward and poised to strike for the ball when it is put in, but still in a position to give a forward push to the scrum. You can see that Bobby's shoulders are a few inches higher than the level of his bottom. There are two reasons for this. First, this helps him withstand all the pressure exerted on him by the opposition pack. Second, it gives his right leg more freedom of movement to strike for the ball when it is put in. For my part, I hold the ball exactly as I would in a match – at the angle I intend the ball to hit the ground to give Bobby the best chance of a clean, controlled strike.

Once I feed the ball at the right speed to the correct spot and make sure it hits the ground at the same angle it left my hands, it is up to Bobby to strike diagonally across with his right foot to make contact with the ball as it hits the ground (1/2). He hooks the ball with the inside of his right foot as it touches the ground. According to a strict interpretation of the laws it is illegal to strike for the ball until it hits the ground, but in practice this is unworkable. I have played rugby all over the

1/1 △   1/2 ▽

world and hookers strike for the ball the moment it is fed into the scrum, which allows them to hook the ball as it hits the ground.

As Bobby strikes the ball (1/3) he also tries to guide it accurately back into the second row of the scrum for a good, controlled heel; to do this it is important that he follows through with his right foot after he has struck the ball (1/4).

Bobby Windsor is a past master of the art of hooking and he feels there are several important points for young players to remember. They must develop a perfect understanding with their scrum-half. The ball must only be put in when the scrum is steady and the hooker is ready. Intense concentration is essential all the time and he must keep his eyes on the ball from the moment the scrum-half prepares to feed the ball until he has successfully hooked it. He needs quick reflexes and should develop a smooth hooking rhythm so the ball is swept back in a controlled manner. The moment that has been achieved, he should resume a scrummaging position and add his weight and strength to help the general stability of the scrum.

1/3 △

1/4 ▽

FRONT ROW

As I have already said, I was very fortunate to have played most of my career behind outstanding scrummaging packs. That meant, first and foremost, a tight, solid front row. The props must bind tightly on the hooker and give him every support. The props bind with their inside arms round the hooker's waist, gripping very firmly with their hands on either the lower part of his jersey or the top of his shorts. The hooker binds with his arms over the shoulders of his props and he then grips their jerseys tightly just under their outside arms (2/1 and 2). The whole front row should be so tight and solid that each lock should have to make a conscious effort to get his head between the prop and the hooker.

In order that the hooker can be as near the ball as possible on his own put-in, he should be as close as possible to his loose-head prop (2/3). The loose-head prop should have his feet fairly wide apart with his left leg slightly in front of his right leg. The hooker can then guide the ball back between the legs of the loose-head prop. The loose-head prop binds on his opponent by gripping his jersey tightly with his left hand. His head should be underneath his opponent's chin or on his chest. His back should be straight and flat to allow his hooker a clear view of the put-in. His head should be held up and he should be trying to look straight ahead and not at the ground. Both loose-head and tight-head props should scrummage with a straight, flat back to help them transmit the drive from their own scrum, and also to absorb and withstand the pressure exerted on them from the opposition pack (2/4).

LOCKS

The locks are the engine-room of the scrum. They provide crucial strength, power and muscle. Like the front row, they must bind tightly together, gripping very firmly their partner's shorts with their inside arm (2/5). The

2/1 △   2/2 ▽

△ 2/3

△ 2/4

taller player (in this case Allan Martin) will generally bind with his arm over his partner's (2/6). As they approach the front row, they bind together (2/7), go down behind the front row together (2/8) and each place one knee on the ground ready to drive forward when the whole scrum goes down (2/9). The front five forwards should go down into the scrummage together as a unit. Indeed, ideally, all eight forwards should pack down together at every scrum to achieve maximum efficiency. The locks bind on their props with their outside arm between the prop's legs and they grip firmly on to the top of the prop's shorts (2/9).

Both locks scrummage with their legs about shoulder-width apart, well back and slightly bent at the knees so that they can be straightened when the ball is put in to transmit maximum power. The locks should have straight, flat backs, just like the props. To help keep this position, their heads should always be held up with their eyes looking forward. Some locks, like the right lock here, prefer to scrummage with only their toes dug into the ground to gain the best purchase for a strong

2/5

2/6

forward drive. Others, like the left lock here, prefer the whole of the inside of their feet to be in contact with the ground (2/10). It is simply a case of personal preference. The lock's shoulders should be pushing under the buttocks of the players in front.

2/7 △   2/8 ▽

2/9 ▽

12

▽2/11 △2/10

▽2/12

BACK ROW

The number eight joins the scrum forcing his head between the two locks, pushing hard with his shoulders on their buttocks and binding tightly with his arms round their legs and gripping their shorts.

The left flanker binds with his right arm over the left lock, his right hand firmly gripping the lock's jersey. Similarly, the right flanker binds on the right lock, gripping his jersey tightly with his left hand (2/11 and 12).

Both flankers can give their props great assistance by packing down at a slight angle and pushing with their shoulders on the top of the thigh of the prop's outside leg. This helps the prop absorb the pressure from the opposition pack and gives him the solidity he needs to give his hooker full support. The flanker will usually push with his outside leg in front of his other leg as you can see Terry Cobner doing here (2/12).

The three back-row players should scrummage with straight, flat backs, their heads help up and legs slightly bent so that they can straighten them when the ball is put in and thus transmit an instant forward drive.

3/1

3/2

CHANNEL ONE POSSESSION

With the scrum now tightly bound and rock solid, the hooker in a comfortable position with a clear view of the ball in the scrum-half's hands and the other seven forwards ready to give him every assistance, it is time to put the ball in (3/1).

As I put it in, the hooker whips his right foot diagonally across to the spot where the ball lands. At the same time, the props must not yield an inch, keeping their legs anchored to the ground and driving forwards and upwards into the opposition front row. Simultaneously, the other five forwards, still binding tightly together, must all drive aggressively forward by straightening both legs, transmitting every ounce of their strength and power in a forward drive. It is clearly important the whole pack work together as a unit. Only regular scrummaging practice at training sessions will develop the rhythm and cohesion that is vital to turn eight individual forwards into a smooth well-oiled machine who will work together in perfect harmony.

As the ball is struck by the hooker, I begin to move behind my left flanker (3/2). For this

3/3

3/4

type of quick heel, the flanker packs down at an angle of 45°, which means it is easier for the ball to come out and at the same time harder for the opposition scrum-half to get at me (3/3).

The moment the ball is out, I must be in a position to pick it up and pass to the fly-half in one movement (3/4). This possession, which is known as a 'channel one' heel, I have always found useful when my pack has been under a lot of pressure and has been driven backwards, wheeled or generally disrupted. This heel is so quick, it doesn't give the opposition pack a chance to disrupt my forwards. It is also useful when my side is on the attack and we want a fast heel to unleash the backs quickly.

In 1980, most teams playing against the mighty England pack would have been well advised to try channel one heeling. Ireland, with a quicksilver scrum-half like Colin Paterson, might well have been able to make good use of this type of possession. Of course, the great disadvantage of channel one is the ball arrives in the scrum-half's hands only fractionally before the arrival of the opposition scrum-half, so it does demand very sharp reflexes and great concentration.

CHANNEL TWO POSSESSION

For much greater control, most packs that I played behind, certainly Cardiff, Wales and the Lions, used 'channel two'. This demands that the scrum remains rock solid after the ball is hooked and it is a little slower than a channel one heel, but it does give the scrum-half much greater protection and, in general, I much prefer it.

The hooker sweeps the ball back between the loose-head prop's legs as before (4/1). But this time the flanker is not packing at such a wide angle. He is binding much closer to the left lock and directly behind the loose-head prop, which makes it easier for him to guide the ball across to the feet of the left lock (4/2). The left lock pushes it from his left foot across to his right and then pushes it back to the feet of the number eight (4/3). The number eight releases the ball beside his right foot whenever the scrum-half wants it (4/4).

There is no way any of the opposition can spoil the scrum-half as they can't get anywhere near him. I must say I enjoyed playing behind the sort of pack who could give me this kind of possession whenever I wanted it.

4/1

4/2

4/3

4/4

OPPOSITION PUT-IN

So far, I have only dealt with my own put-in to the scrum. But in roughly half the scrums in each match the opposition will have the put-in. It is very important on these occasions to subject their pack and scrum-half to as much pressure as possible and make it as difficult as possible for the opposition to unleash their backs with quick, controlled possession. There are three principal ways of disrupting the other scrum. The best is a quick strike against the head, but this is by far the hardest and, unless your side has an exceptionally good hooker, not something to be tried too often. By all means have a go early on, but if this is unsuccessful it would be best to concentrate on an eight-man shove where every member of your pack works together to try and push the opposition off the ball. Even if the opposition heels the ball but, at the same time, is being driven backwards at a rate of knots, it gives me a wonderful opportunity to destroy the other scrum-half and spoil his possession. It is possible to inject further variety by occasionally wheeling the scrum as soon as the ball is put in. Once again, I can put pressure on the other scrum-half when the ball eventually squirts out of the side of the scrum.

BACK-ROW MOVES

Continuing this theme of keeping the utmost pressure on the opposition at all times, it is vital to perfect one or two back-row moves when you win your own put-in. Apart from at worst setting up good second-phase possession with the opposing backrow totally committed, this sort of variety keeps the other side guessing at every scrum. Their back row must always wait to check there is no back-row move being attempted against them before they can get on with their normal defensive and covering duties. They can't fly round the field until the scrum-half has passed, which gives your back division a little more time and room in which to operate.

5/1 △   5/2 ▽

5/3 ▽

△5/4

▽5/5

Back-row moves should not be overdone and should only be attempted from controlled channel two possession (5/1). On a given signal the right flanker (in this case Jeff Squire) breaks up and immediately sweeps round past the scrum-half (5/2). With the opposition scrum-half on top of me, I can still give a short, quick pass to the flanker (5/3). He continues round the scrum and heads straight towards the opposition (5/4). On driving into their back row, he can feed his own left flanker (Terry Cobner) (5/5). This player may break through the opposition (5/6). Or he may just set up a maul which his side should win, with the opposing back row all sucked into the maul and unable to cover.

▽5/6

From another back-row move, the scrum-half can be released on a break. Again it is essential to win the channel two ball (6/1 and 2). The number eight (Jeff Squire) moves the ball to his right foot (6/3). As I run away from the scrum, he picks up and in one movement flicks a short pass to me (6/4 and 5). I set off, hopefully, outside the opposition back row towards their back division (6/6).

6/1

6/2

6/3

6/4

6/5

6/6

In a simple variation on the above move, again from channel two ball (7/1 and 2), the number eight (Jeff Squire) moves the ball to his right foot (7/3). On a given signal he breaks from the scrum as I go for the ball (7/4). I feed him with a short, quick pass (7/5) and he drives straight towards the opposition (7/6).

7/1 △   7/2 ▽

7/3 ▽

▽ 7/5 △ 7/4

▽ 7/6

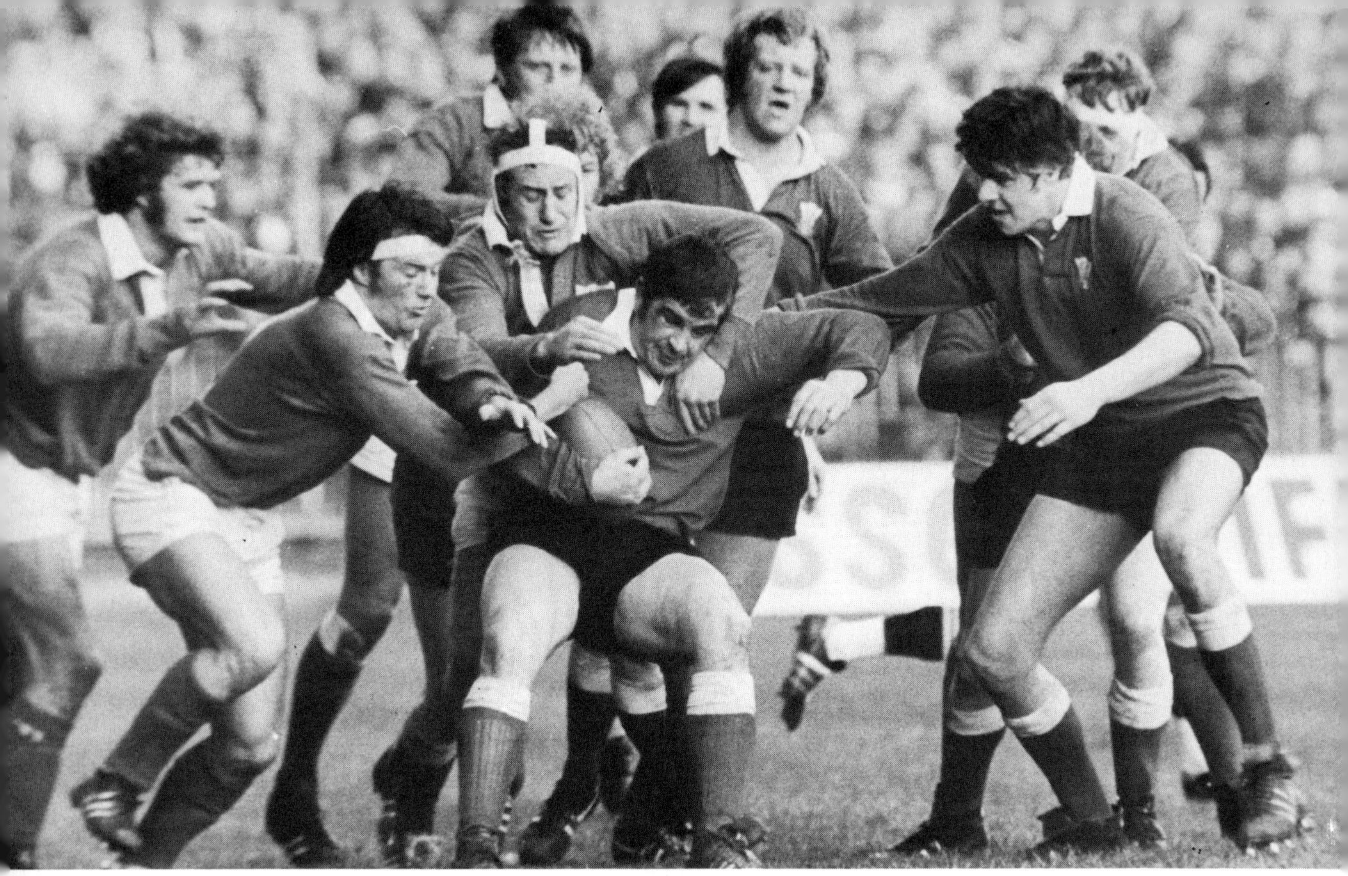

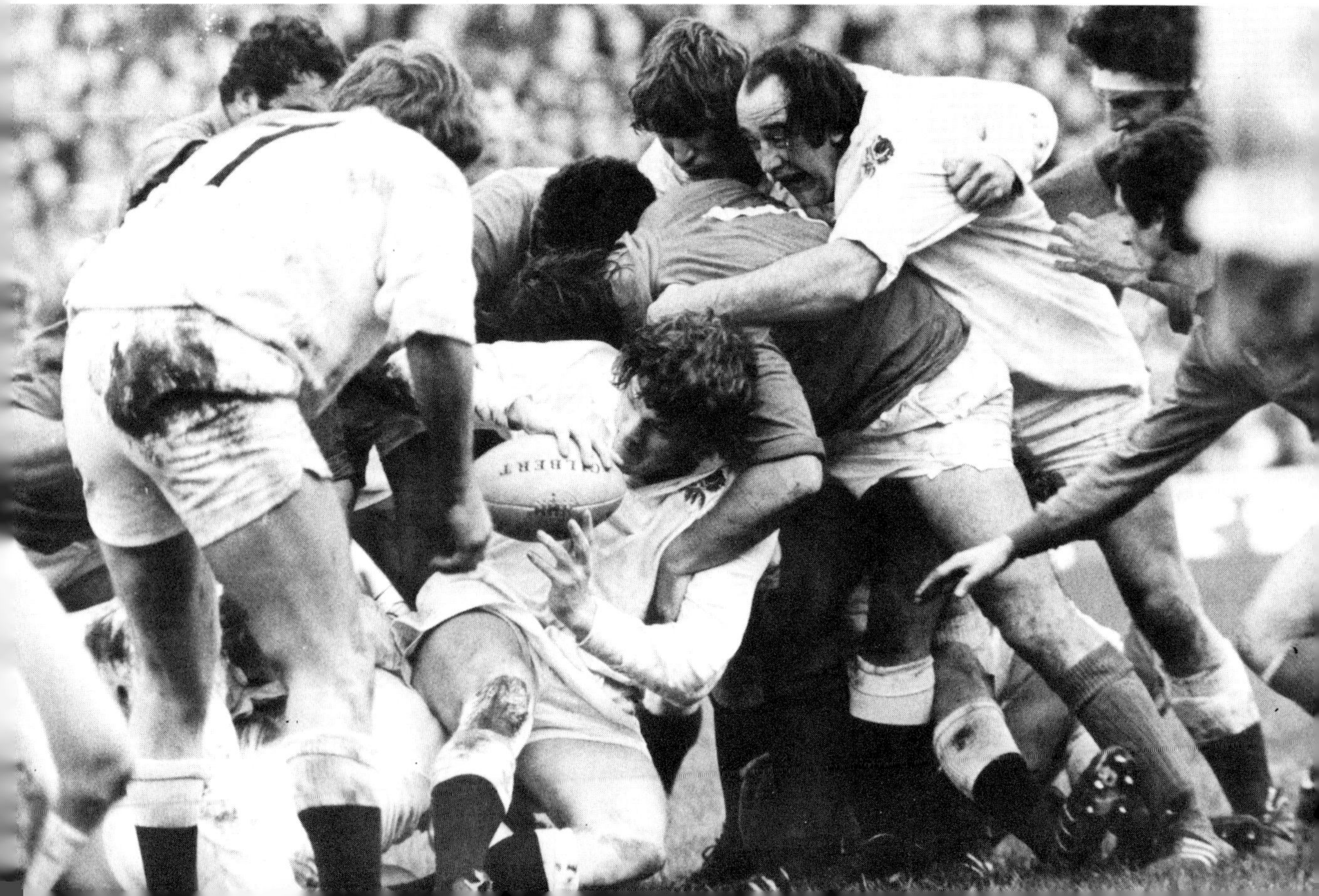

2 THE RUCK AND MAUL

In internationals not many tries are scored directly from set-piece possession because at that level defences are so well organized it takes a stroke of genius to breach the defence or create an overlap and then beat the cover. Of course it does happen occasionally, but it is much more usual for tries to come from second-phase possession. In the loose, the opposition defence is not nearly so well organized and they may well have some of their back row or even a key member of the threequarter line buried at the bottom of the ruck or maul. The higher the standard of rugby in which I played, the harder it was to score from set-piece play, but, at the same time, it was vital to win good first-phase possession because that made it very much easier to win the loose ball.

If my pack were on top in the scrums and the line-out, as the '74 Lions always were, then it was virtually certain we would also be in control of the loose ball. I believe that good scrummage ball should be used mainly for gaining ground, with one of the half-backs kicking for position or for setting up really good rucks or mauls in order to win the second-phase ball and then run at the opposition. It was this running from broken play that made the '71 and '74 Lions so outstanding and it also stood Wales in pretty good stead throughout the seventies.

Set-piece possession is vital, but often as a means to an end rather than an end in itself. It is far easier to win a ruck or maul if your team has set it up in the first place.

The first chapter has dealt with the different techniques needed to win the good set-piece ball. I have stressed the need to avoid becoming predictable during a match; if the opposition can guess what you are going to do, it is far easier for them to defend against you. Always have plenty of options and bring variety to your game. From scrums you can use channel one or two possession depending on the circumstances and indulge in a whole variety of back-row moves to keep the opposition guessing. This makes it harder for them to defend and allows you, at worst, to set up perfect ruck or maul situations. Similarly, variety at the line-out is very important, whether you use the peel, the throw over the top, or shortened line-out variations with two, three or four players in the line.

After winning the ball, you can set up a ruck or maul on your own terms, either with four forwards driving into the opposition from a peel or throw over the top, or by using a crash ball in mid-field. You should always win the loose ball in these situations and can then launch a second and more dangerous attack against a depleted and disorganized defence.

Bobby Windsor setting up a maul for Wales against Ireland in 1975 with Allan Martin ready to support him

Fran Cotton in the act of feeding the ball from a maul during the England–France match in 1975

THE RUCK

Initially, the most important person is the player carrying the ball. He must drive into the tackle but at the same time make certain he doesn't lose control of the ball. If it is knocked out of his hands in the tackle then it becomes a fifty-fifty ball which the opposition is just as likely to win. Here, Jeff Squire runs towards the opposition (8/1) and by lowering his shoulder and sinking his hip into him he takes out the first defender as he drives into the tackle (8/2). Jeff is in complete control of the ball as he goes down and he can place the ball on the ground as he does so (8/3). He must then release his hand immediately or he will be penalized. By placing the ball on the ground, he makes it an easy stationary target on which his support players can focus as they thunder into the ruck. If he rolls it back as he goes down, it is quite likely one of the advancing support players will kick it forward by mistake and thus lose control.

It is imperative that the support players arrive as quickly as possible and, at very worst, at least as fast as the opposition. If the ruck is being set up from good set-piece possession, it is likely your team will be going forward into the ruck and so your forwards should arrive first. The first players should bind together and drive vigorously over the players on the ground (8/3)

8/1 △   8/2 ▽

8/3 ▽

▽8/5   △8/4

▽8/6

staying on their feet and ignoring the ball completely (8/4). They shouldn't start trying to heel the ball as, ideally, the ball should stay exactly where it is. Their job is to get over the ball and protect it from the opposition. If they arrive well before the opposition they can of course pick up the ball and continue the attack, but on this occasion they have only arrived a split second before the other side and are intent on setting up a solid platform to ensure they will secure the rucked ball. The speed with which the rest of the forwards arrive is crucial as it will be their added drive, impetus and momentum which will steam-roller the opposition back a metre (8/5) and leave the ball free for the scrum-half to collect (8/6). Once the first player has been tackled and the ball put on the ground it is vital that the rest of the forwards arrive in as great a number, and as fast, as possible. They must drive aggressively into the ruck, hit it low and hard, stay on their feet and move the opposition backwards.

If any player carrying the ball is knocked to the ground, a ruck will inevitably develop. But sometimes, if a player remains on his feet in the tackle, his side may still prefer rucking to mauling. In this case, as soon as his initial support arrives, he can put the ball on the ground for the rest of his pack to drive over. Often a fast, but light, pack may find it much more effective to ruck rather than maul. If they are up against a big, strong pack, they may well find if they try to maul every time that they are just not strong enough to keep possession of the ball. They can have the ball ripped out of their grasp by sheer strength and weight, and a light quick pack may often be better advised to concentrate on rucking. When the ball-carrier drives into the opposition, as his first support players arrive, he can lay the ball on the ground. The rest of the forwards should arrive as fast as possible, hit the ruck low and hard, stay on their feet and drive over the ball. If their drive is halted, they can then heel the ball back. In either situation, it is very difficult for the opposition to interfere and spoil your possession as long as your pack is ruthlessly determined and aggressive, and arrives first and in sufficient numbers.

Another great advantage of rucked ball is that it happens so quickly. If your team has a good fast back division then it is great to win a quick rucked ball. One moment one of your players is setting up a ruck – the very next moment the ball is pinging along your threequarter line with the opposition back row committed in the ruck. This was used to tremendous effect by the Lions in 1971 and 1974 and I can vividly remember the Lions scoring over twenty tries on each of those tours direct from superb rucked ball. Terry Cobner says that much the same thing happened with the Lions in 1977.

A rolling maul during a British Lions match in New Zealand in 1977. The Lions have set up a maul but instead of feeding the ball back to the scrum-half Derek Quinnell rolls off and charges towards the opposition with Jeff Squire, Billy Beaumont, Bobby Windsor and Graham Price ready to follow in support

9/1

THE MAUL

Many of the important ingredients of a good ruck also apply to the maul. The ball carrier must protect the ball at all times and he desperately relies on the speed of his support. As Jeff Squire is about to drive in to the opposition, he dips his shoulder and turns side on to the defender to protect the ball (9/1 and 2). The moment he thunders into the defender, Jeff whips his body round so that his back is now facing the opposition and he holds the ball quite low in outstretched arms to make it extremely difficult, if not impossible, for the opposition to interfere with the ball. Jeff has adopted a half-squat stance and his feet are more than shoulder-width apart to give him a really solid base (9/3). Without this secure platform, the fate of the maul would be in some doubt. The next prerequisite is the speed with which the support players arrive. The first *two* must arrive before, or at the same time as, the first two of the opposition. Now there is a school of thought which believes the first support player to arrive should take the ball to protect it. Neither I, Terry Cobner nor Jeff Squire subscribe to this view.

The great Welsh club sides like Pontypool (there hasn't been a better club pack in recent years), and indeed the Welsh international side, firmly believe the first two players to arrive should bind together and drive over the top of the ball-carrier and bind firmly on his back, giving him rock solid support, one on either side of him (9/4 and 5). The opposition will find it very difficult, but not actually impossible, to get at the ball now – it is very well protected. The next players to arrive explode into the maul on either side of the ball-carrier and their added impetus should give the maul even greater stability (9/6 and 7). But they must arrive to support Jeff Squire as quickly as possible. All seven supporting forwards should remain on their feet, bind tightly together, with straight backs as in a scrummage, to absorb fully any pressure from the opposition. When the scrum-half sees all the opposition are committed to the maul, he can call for the ball and unleash his backs (9/8). Support players should make sure they don't get in the way of the ball-carrier and obstruct his pass to the scrum-half.

9/2

9/3

9/4

31

9/5 △   9/6 ▽

▽9/8 △9/7

10/1

10/2

There is one very important little refinement to this type of maul which has proved very useful and effective to teams like Pontypool, Cardiff and Wales over the years. Once a side has mastered the simple, basic maul, they should automatically progress to this extra refinement. Even though the first method is pretty secure, if the opposition happen to arrive in greater numbers and quicker than your support players, they can still disrupt your possession by pulling an arm of the ball-carrier or by generally interfering with him. The very best Welsh club packs, including Pontypool, and the national side have overcome this problem with the same sort of sophisticated technique we will see again later in the book in the maul which develops at a line-out. The simple guidelines Pontypool have adopted mean the first two players in support bind over the back of the ball-carrier as before (10/1). But the third support player to arrive – in

10/3

10/4

this case Terry Cobner — always takes the ball from the ball-carrier (10/2). The rest of the forwards explode into the maul as before (10/3). The ball is now completely protected. It is absolutely impossible for the opposition to get anywhere near it. Whenever the scrum-half wants the ball it can be fed to him, and he can whip it out to the backs (10/4). Like Pontypool, Wales and the 1974 British Lions, I firmly believe this is by far the best method of mauling and I would strongly recommend all teams to adopt it. After ten years' playing international rugby all over the world, I have seen a great variety of styles, but none to beat this simple system. And it is simple — every team, at every level, can and should do it. It has been a great pleasure to play scrum-half behind the packs who have mauled in this way. And it has led directly to a host of spectacular tries at club and international level.

11/1

11/2

ROLLING MAUL

I've already emphasized the importance of variety in the game, and it is well worthwhile mentioning here the fluid or rolling maul. it can be devastatingly effective, as the 1980 British Lions showed in South Africa, first to set up a maul, commit all the opposition forwards to it, and then, when they expect the ball to be fed out to the backs, they discover instead that your forwards peel off the maul to continue the attack themselves. Like all the best things in rugby, it requires a great amount of practice to perfect this little manoeuvre, but it should prove to be well within the capabilities of most sides. In this sequence, Jeff Squire drives into the opposition

36

11/3

11/4

to set up a maul (11/1 and 2). As he turns to make the ball available to his own side, the first two support players bind over him to give him maximum initial protection (11/3). Terry Cobner arrives next and takes the ball, but this time, instead of preparing to feed the scrum-half, he rolls off the maul and, helped by one of his team-mates, drives once again at the opposition (11/4). Already you can see Jeff heading off in support and, with the rest of the forwards in pursuit, a dangerous attack can be mounted. If and when the opposition manages to check this move, the ball can either be fed back from the subsequent maul or the forwards can roll off again. As with other ploys and variations, it increases your options.

37

FALLING ON THE BALL

Finally in this section, it is important to remember that it is sometimes necessary to ruck or maul for the ball on the retreat. It is far easier to win the loose ball going forward, but it is just as important to be able to kill the loose ball in a defensive situation. With this in mind every player in the team should be able to fall on the ball and be ready to set up a maul on the retreat.

First of all, it is essential to keep your eyes on the rolling ball all the time (12/1). As Jeff Squire reaches the ball, he falls on it with his back to the opposition (12/2 and 3).

12/1 △   12/2 ▽

12/3 ▽

In the same movement as he goes down on the ball he should try to bounce back up on his feet, making quite sure that he has the ball completely under control (12/4). As he gets up, he adopts the same position as he would for a maul – half-crouching, back to the opposition, and feet wide apart to form a solid base. At the same time his first two support players should arrive and bind firmly over his back, one on each side to give him maximum protection (12/5). The rest of the forwards join in as they did in the maul situation and the ball is fed back to the scrum-half (12/6).

△12/4

12/5▽

▽12/6

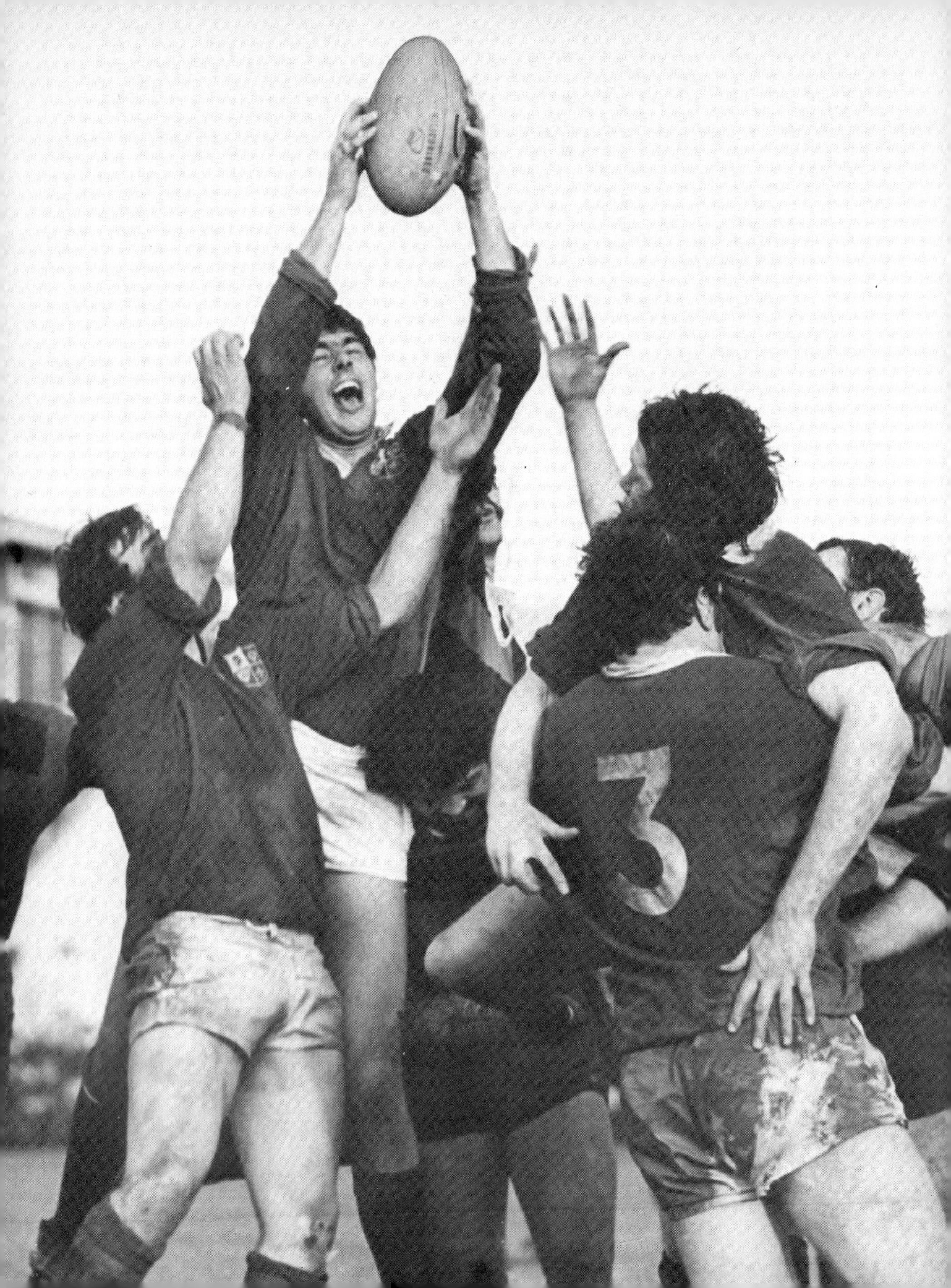

3 THE LINE-OUT

The two most important people at a line-out are the jumper and the person throwing in the ball, but all the other forwards have to do everything in their power to help and protect the jumper and to tidy up the ball if it is not caught cleanly. Usually nowadays, the hooker throws in, which allows the wing to stay 10 metres back to make an extra man in attack if his side wins the line-out and an extra man in defence if the opposition wins the ball.

The best two players I have seen in recent years at throwing-in are Bobby Windsor of Wales and Peter Wheeler of England. It takes a tremendous amount of practice to perfect the art of throwing-in, but it is a vital skill to master and it can make all the difference to a jumper. Accuracy is the first essential. Different jumpers will prefer the ball to travel at varying speeds and some will like it to be lobbed, others to be thrown with a fast, low trajectory. But whatever speed, height and elevation are demanded by the jumper, the basic action of the thrower-in is the same.

A superb two-handed catch at the line-out by Allan Martin for the British Lions against Canterbury in New Zealand in 1977

THE THROW-IN

As Bobby Windsor demonstrates here he stands with his left leg forward and with the ball held in both hands (13/1). He then points the ball towards the line-out, still holding it in both hands, and concentrates on his target area so he knows exactly where he is aiming (13/2). With

13/3

13/4

his eyes. still firmly fixed on his target, he leans gently back and prepares to throw in the ball, now held in his right hand (13/3). In a smooth flowing movement he rolls forward and throws the ball in one continuous action. His right hand turns slightly over and follows straight through to impart the spinning, torpedo action which is the hallmark of a good throw (13/4).

13/3

13/4

JUMPING TECHNIQUES

There are four main types of line-out possession which budding locks should practise. And with lots of practice they may one day be as good as British Lion Allan Martin who demonstrates his skills here. The best, but the most difficult, is the two-handed catch (14/1). This gives the jumper the most control and is the most easily protected possession. At a two-man line-out where spoiling and interference from the opposition is likely to be minimal, it is possible to catch two-handed and simultaneously feed the ball to the scrum-half (14/2, 3 and 4). This is more accurate and controlled than palming.

For the jumper standing at the front of the line-out, the low hard throw about shoulder height contains the element of surprise (14/5). If the jumper takes one step forward as the hooker releases the ball, he should have caught the ball before his opposite number has had time to move.

Finally, it is possible to reach that little bit higher by jumping with one hand for the ball (14/6 and 7). But, as Allan is quick to emphasize, it is essential to be certain you know where your scrum-half is and to palm the ball straight to him. It is inviting disaster simply to leap up and slap the ball back anywhere. It must be carefully guided towards the scrum-half.

And, just as the scrum-half and hooker must spend time at every training session practising the put-in to the scrum, so too each line-out jumper must spend time at every session practising with the thrower-in until they are working together in perfect harmony.

14/1

14/5

14/2 14/3 14/4

14/6 14/7

TWO-HANDED CATCH

Allan Martin is one of the best line-out jumpers in the world and a great advocate of the two-handed catch. This is the tidiest, most controlled possession and has the added advantage that the backs must stay 10 metres away until the ball is released, which gives them more room to exploit their running skills. Allan likes to jump at four in the line-out and stands side-on to the opposition so that once he has caught the ball he can complete the turn in mid-air to land with his back to the enemy (15/1 and 2). The most important skills Allan brings to jumping are determination and aggression to win the ball, and intense concentration all the time it is in the air with his eyes fixed on the ball.

The jumper must have strong legs and arms and sharp reflexes to react quickly to every situation. Once he has caught the ball and landed with his back to the opposition, he must receive instant support from the players immediately in front of, and behind, him. They bind over the top of the jumper, one on either side, to give him complete protection from the opposition. Simultaneously, the other forwards should bind together to form a solid platform with no gaps for the opposition to come through and disrupt possession (15/3). From this stable base the pack can either drive forward or release the ball to the scrum-half (15/4). Allan reckons the best two-handed middle of the line-out jumpers he has ever played against are Nigel Horton of England and All Black Andy Haden. Both are explosive, aggressive jumpers with fast reactions who added plenty of variety to their jumping as well as perfect timing, balance and coordination.

15/1 △   15/2 ▽

15/3 △   15/4 ▽

One very popular variation on the standard method shown on the previous page is for the hooker, after he has thrown the ball in, to join the line-out and take the ball from the jumper. After Allan Martin has won the line-out (16/1 and 2), Bobby Windsor smuggles the ball from Allan (16/3 and 4) and then feeds the scrum-half whenever he wants the ball (16/5 and 6). This variation has the added advantage of even more control and greater protection because the ball is that much further away from the opposition. We saw this same sophisticated technique demonstrated in the maul earlier in the book.

16/1 △   16/2 ▽

16/3 ▽

▽16/5   △16/4

▽16/6

PALMING

The crucial point about palming or deflecting from a line-out is accuracy. The jumper must be aware exactly where his scrum-half is standing and he must make sure he guides the ball straight down to him (17/1 and 2). The great advantage of a quick controlled deflected ball is its speed. A split second after the ball has been thrown into the line-out the scrum-half can be whipping it out to the fly-half to unleash the backs. The opposition back row are caught flat-footed and the opposition backs are still 10 metres behind the line-out. As Allan Martin always says, and I would just like to emphasize, if palming from a line-out is well done, with speed, accuracy and complete control, it is outstanding possession of the highest quality. But if it is slapped wildly back, it is disastrous and dangerous. The opposition can come pouring through the moment the ball is tapped out of the line-out and, if it is doesn't go straight to the scrum-half, the end product is likely to be

17/1

17/2

chaos. And I can assure you it is a nightmare for the scrum-half.

The best exponents of an accurately palmed ball I played with were Allan Martin, Delme Thomas and Mervyn Davies of Wales, Gordon Brown of Scotland and Ken Goodall of Ireland. They all took the greatest care to give me the best possible possession.

TWO-HANDED CATCH AT THE FRONT

Almost as quick, and with much greater control, is the two-handed catch at the front from a fast throw (18/1). As the ball is caught, in the same movement it is transferred from over the head of the catcher straight to the scrum-half (18/2). This is quick, quality possession, but it is a very difficult technique to master and should initially only be attempted by a very tall line-out jumper, who can comfortably outjump his opponents.

18/1

18/2

19/1

19/2

Always remember to vary your play. Allan Martin stresses the need to keep the opposition guessing at all times on your own throw-in. Sometimes he catches two-handed, holds the ball and drives forward, and sometimes he catches two-handed and delivers the ball instantly 'off the top' from the line-out to the scrum-half. Sometimes he palms or deflects one-handed. On some occasions, he jumps straight up in the air, while at other times he will take one step forward and then take off. He can also signal to the thrower-in with a nod of his head or a hand signal that he wants the ball thrown in faster or slower, higher or lower, a little deeper so he takes a step back and jumps, or a little shorter so he takes a step forward before he jumps. Always make it hard for the opposition to know not only where the throw-in is going but also how the ball will travel through the air. Their main aim at your throw-in to the line-out will be to spoil your possession if they can't outjump you. The more variety you inject into your play the more difficult life will be for the opposition to interfere with you.

SHORT THROW TO THE FRONT

The short, hard throw to the front of the line-out is used mostly in defensive situations. This is because it is often easier to win the ball at the front, but it is not quite so useful for the backs to launch a running attack. A ball won in the middle or the back of a line-out is more useful for the backs because the fly-half and his threequarters will be that much further away from the opposition back row. However, if the main preoccupation is simply to clear your lines, a ball taken at two in the line-out is good enough.

The advantage for the jumper at the front is the element of surprise, as I mentioned at the beginning of this chapter.

The moment the ball leaves the hooker's hand as he fires it into the line-out, your jumper, knowing this is going to happen, can take one step forward and pluck the ball out of the air at shoulder height, leaving his opposite number flat-footed (19/1). As Allan Martin jumps, he

19/3

19/4

can also turn his back on the opposition, which means when he lands the ball will be protected (19/2). He still requires quick support from his colleagues on either side (19/3). With the rest of the forwards quickly adding their support and sealing any gaps to make sure the opposition can't burst through, the ball can either be slipped to the hooker as in sequence 16 or delivered straight back to the scrum-half (19/4).

This type of throw may look easy enough, but in fact it is the hardest sort of ball for a jumper to win and it requires a tremendous amount of practice, and perfect timing and coordination between the thrower-in and the jumper. There were several great exponents of this particular skill in the ten years I played international rugby. The names which spring to mind – Ireland's Willie John McBride, Geoff Wheel of Wales, England's Billy Beaumont and, possibly the best of them all, Springbok Frik du Preez. He was only just over six feet tall but he didn't often get beaten when he jumped at the front of a South African line-out.

THE PEEL

The peel is a very effective way of varying line-out play during a match and if done well can cause the opposition all sorts of problems. At best, the forwards can drive a gap straight through the other team's threequarters. At worst, your side should set up a perfect ruck or maul to win good second-phase possession, with one or two of the opposition backs and back-row men totally committed and temporarily out of the game. I must say that second-phase ball after a peel was always fabulous possession for me and my backs, and on countless occasions it led to tries. This was true with Cardiff, Wales and the Lions.

The throw will go to either the last or (preferably) the second last player in the line-out – in this case, to Jeff Squire. He palms it accurately down to one of his props. This player will have detached himself from the front of the line as soon as the ball has passed over him and he will sprint along the line to be in a position to take the deflection (20/1). Ideally the deflection should be guided diagonally out into the open spaces for the prop to catch and charge straight over the gain line (20/2). He can then drive flat out towards the opposition threequarter line with his own forwards streaming along in support (20/3). If he is tackled by the back row the moment he rounds the line-out, he can feed the ball to the next supporting forward who can continue to launch the attack. The palm must be accurate, the prop must have good hands, plenty of speed and power, and the support must be fast and plentiful.

20/2

20/3

There is one simple variation of the peel which I liked to be involved in as it gave me quick line-out ball and a bit of room in which to move. Just as for the peel, the ball is thrown long to the back of the line where the penultimate player (Jeff Squire) palms it down diagonally at an angle of about 45° to the touchline (21/1 and 2). By deflecting it at this angle, I can take it outside the last player of each side in the line out. I can take the ball whilst sprinting flat out and should, as a scrum-half, be able, from this launching pad, to outstrip the opposition back-row (21/3). At this point, as I cross the gain line, I can go for a break on my own, link up with my backs, who should have an overlap with me in the line as an extra man, or feed it back to my supporting forwards to let them thunder on into the opposition backs.

21/1

21/3

22/1

22/2

This move can also be done with a four-man line-out and in this case I like the fourth man (Allan Martin here) to palm the ball back (22/1). Once again, he should deflect it at an angle which allows me to take it on the burst outside the end of the line-out (22/2). At this point I have several options open to me. I can have a go myself, link up with my backs, or feed the forwards who didn't take part in the line-out and they could set up a ruck or maul in midfield. Near the opposition line, I have often burst over to score myself. I shall always remember in one of the toughest games I ever played – Cardiff against Pontypool in the quarter final of the Welsh Cup in 1977 – I scored one of the softest tries of my career. Trailing 10–6 towards the end of the match, Cardiff called a four-man line-out near the Pontypool line. We threw to the back man, he palmed to me and I crashed over before Pontypool realized what had happened. That memorable but incredibly simple try won the match. It was proof, if proof were needed, that variation at the line-out is essential. No team or jumper should become too predictable.

TWO-MAN LINE-OUT

The effectiveness of the two-man line-out has never been better demonstrated to me than by playing against the Japanese. Their forwards are always dwarfed by their opponents at international level, but by a phenomenal speed of thought and by an infinite variety of ploys they often win their full share of line-out ball.

Every team with a small pack of forwards, from schoolboy level upwards, can take great heart from the brilliant exploits of recent Japanese teams.

They bring so much variety to their line-out play, the only thing you can be sure of is that they won't make each throw-in a straightforward jumping contest between two players. That contest they would usually lose. But a two-man line-out is a very different thing. Every Japanese side I've played against or watched has had a quicksilver scrum-half. I remember being caught on the hop myself when they called a two-man line against Wales at Osaka in 1975. Both their forwards took a quick step forward just as the ball was being thrown in. Sensing a fast throw to the front, both Welsh jumpers shot forward to counter such a throw and, as I stood watching all this, the ball soared over the top and their scrum-half flashed past the back of the line-out, caught the ball and sprinted down the field. A great move if your team has small forwards, a good thrower-in and a fast scrum-half.

Japan with five men in the line-out are able to outjump France who only have four men in the line, by throwing to their unmarked man

Another line-out in the France–Japan match at Bordeaux in 1973 shows the Japanese jumper at a three-man line-out taking a quick step forward and getting his hand to the ball before his opponents have realized what has happened

THROW OVER THE TOP

The fact that I've demonstrated this ploy here (23/1–4) with two great jumpers in Allan Martin and Jeff Squire would, I think, greatly appeal to the quick-thinking Japanese. Who would imagine with these two athletic giants standing in the line that they would be totally ignored and the ball thrown over the top. The element of surprise is again evident.

23/1

23/2

23/3

23/4

24/1

24/2

24/3

24/4

Usually a two-man line-out is called because the other team have taller players and are outjumping you even on your own throw-in. This means you don't really want a straight up-and-down jumping contest as your men will probably lose. Here, Allan Martin stands at the front about 8 metres from the touchline with Jeff Squire behind him (24/1). As the ball is about to leave the hand of the thrower-in, Allan steals the initiative by taking a rapid step forward, leaving his opposite number flat-footed, or at any rate a fraction behind him (24/2). At the same time, Allan explodes into the air to catch a fast, low throw (24/3), and before his opponent can do anything about it he has fed the scrum-half (24/4). Speed of thought and action win most two-man line-outs, but, as always, timing and coordination are also crucially important.

There is another way the front jumper at a two man line-out can outwit his opposite number. Once again, Allan stands 8 metres from the touchline (25/1). As the hooker takes the ball back behind his head ready to throw in, Allan takes a firm step forward (25/2). Not to be caught out again, as soon as he sees what is happening, his opposite number immediately follows suit and takes a step forward (25/3). But, just as he does this, Allan takes one pace backwards and, at the same time, jumps up to palm a neatly disguised lobbed throw back to the scrum-half (25/4). If done quickly and accurately, there is precious little the opposition can do.

25/1

25/2

25/3

25/4

26/1

26/2

26/3

26/4

In yet another variation, the initial stance is the same (26/1). As the ball is about to be released by the thrower-in, Allan takes a step forward to lure the opposition forward, while, at exactly the same time, Jeff Squire takes a step back (26/2). No sooner has he taken the step back, than he takes off to meet the throw-in and palm it accurately back to the scrum-half (26/3), who can then whip it out to the backs (26/4).

63

I hope that this chapter on line-out play will go a long way to persuading everyone that lock forwards are not just a couple of 6 foot 6 inch robots. Good jumpers have to keep their wits about them at every line-out. They must not be predictable or the opposition will find it fairly easy to spoil their possession. They must develop a sound basic technique and plenty of variety in their play. They need complete harmony with the thrower-in and total concentration at each line-out. They need power, strength, determination, razor-sharp reflexes and a quick mind. Given all these factors and a pack of forwards quick to support the jumper and clean up any untidy ball, then the backs can look forward to some high-quality possession from the line-out.

Allan Martin palming to Gareth Edwards after outjumping Jean-Pierre Bastiat and Jean-Francois Imberon in the Wales–France match in 1977